D0843062

Date: 10/27/21

**J BIO HUSTON
Chandler, Matt,
Nyjah Huston : skateboard
superstar /**

PALM BEACH COUNTY
LIBRARY SYSTEM
3650 SUMMIT BLVD.
WEST PALM BEACH, FL 33406

Sports Illustrated KIDS

STARS OF SPORTS

NYJAH HUSTON

SKATEBOARD SUPERSTAR

by Matt Chandler

Stars of Sports is published by Capstone Press, an imprint of Capstone.
1710 Roe Crest Drive, North Mankato, Minnesota 56003
www.capstonepub.com

Copyright © 2021 by Capstone. All rights reserved. No part of this publication may be reproduced in whole or in part, or stored in a retrieval system, or transmitted in any form or by any means, electronic, mechanical, photocopying, recording, or otherwise, without written permission of the publisher.

SPORTS ILLUSTRATED KIDS is a trademark of ABG-SI LLC. Used with permission.

Library of Congress Cataloging-in-Publication Data

Names: Chandler, Matt, author.
Title: Nyjah Huston : skateboard superstar / by Matt Chandler.
Description: North Mankato : Capstone Press, an imprint of Capstone, [2021] | Series: Sports illustrated kids stars of sports | Includes bibliographical references and index. | Audience: Ages 8-11 | Audience: Grades 4-6 | Summary: "A unique childhood gave Nyjah Huston a unique outlook. Growing up in California and Puerto Rico, Huston started skateboarding when he was just four years old. By age 11, he was competing in the X Games and shocking the skateboarding world with his wild boardslides. Learn how the small kid with the big dreadlocks grew into the highest-paid skateboarder in the world."—Provided by publisher.
Identifiers: LCCN 2020037778 (print) | LCCN 2020037779 (ebook) | ISBN 9781496695260 (hardcover) | ISBN 9781977154682 (pdf) | ISBN 9781977156341 (kindle edition)
Subjects: LCSH: Huston, Nyjah, 1994– —Juvenile literature. | Skateboarders—United States—Biography—Juvenile literature. | Rastafarians—United States—Biography—Juvenile literature.
Classification: LCC GV859.812.H87 C43 2021 (print) | LCC GV859.812.H87 (ebook) | DDC 796.22—dc23
LC record available at https://lccn.loc.gov/2020037778
LC ebook record available at https://lccn.loc.gov/2020037779.

Editorial Credits
Editor: Alison Deering; Designer: Heidi Thompson; Media Researcher: Eric Gohl; Production Specialist: Spencer Rosio

Image Credits
AP Images: Reed Saxon, 11; Getty Images: Harry How, 27, Hyoung Chang, 9, Jeff Gross, 16, Michael Bezjian, 15, 19, Sam Mellish, 25, Stephen Dunn, 20, 21, The Asahi Shimbun, 28; Newscom: Aaron Lavinsky/TNS, 23, Actionplus/Nigel Waldron, Cover, John Walton/ZUMA Press, 7, Kyodo, 5, Speed Media/Icon Sportswire, 24, Steve Boyle/ZUMA Press, 8, 13, Steven K. Doi/ZUMAPRESS, 17; Shutterstock: bbernard, 1

All internet sites appearing in back matter were available and accurate when this book was sent to press.

Direct Quotations
Page 6, from February 27, 2018, Nike News article "Nyjah Huston Nike SB Nyjah," https://news.nike.com
Page 8, from April 8, 2010, video "Nyjah Huston—Dew Tour 2006 Panosnic Open (Interview)", https://www.youtube.com
Page 12, from October 7, 2011, ESPN article "The Nyjah Huston Interview," https://www.espn.com
Page 14, from October 1, 2015, *Rolling Stone* article, "The Impossible Rise of Nyjah Huston," https://www.rollingstone.com
Pages 15 and 16, from September 1, 2015, The Players Tribune article, "Let It Flow," https://www.theplayerstribune.com
Page 20, from July 30, 2011, video "Nyjah Huston Takes Gold in Men's Skateboard Street Final—ESPN X Games," https://www.youtube.com
Page 27, from October 20, 2019, *The Denver Post* article "World Champion Nyjah Huston Heads USA Skateboarding National Team," https://www.denverpost.com

TABLE OF CONTENTS

Glossary terms are **BOLD** on first use.

GOLDEN BOY

In São Paulo, Brazil, the crowd was cheering wildly. It was the final round of the Street League Skateboarding (SLS) 2019 World Championship competition. Nyjah Huston was looking to capture his third title in a row. It would be the sixth of his career.

Huston was in fifth place. Then four of the five skaters before him fell in the third round. Huston had a chance to move up. But it would take a near perfect trick.

Huston launched himself into the air. He spun in a **360** while he flipped his board. He stuck the landing on the rail and rode it off perfectly. The trick earned 9.7 points (out of 10) from the judges. It pushed Huston to second place.

It took two more strong runs to get Huston the gold. His final score was 36.9 (out of 40). Huston had won the gold medal for the third year in a row!

〉〉〉 Huston shows his skill on the board during the SLS 2019 World Championship in São Paulo, Brazil.

RAISED ON A BOARD

Nyjah Huston has been riding a skateboard almost as long as he has been walking. The skating champion was born in Davis, California, on November 30, 1994.

Huston comes from a family of skateboarders. His father, Adeyemi, was a former skateboarder. Growing up, Huston's older brothers skated along with him. His younger brother and sister also skate.

When Huston was young, his family purchased a skate park near their home. Huston spent hours there skating. He wanted to be the best at every trick he did.

He talked about his early love of skateboarding in an interview in 2018. "I was so young, but that's literally all I wanted to do," he said. "I loved it so much. I never wanted to play any other sports. I just wanted to skate every single day."

FACT

Huston's mom, Kelle, homeschooled him and his brothers and sisters. She considered skateboarding part of their schoolwork.

〉〉〉 Huston skates in the men's semifinals during the Street League Skateboarding World Tour in London, England, in 2019.

READY TO COMPETE

Much of Huston's early fame came from videos his dad shot of him doing tricks at local skate parks. But Huston wanted to go pro. To do that, he would have to win some big competitions.

In 2005, Huston won his first title at the Tampa Am in Tampa, Florida. His runs were mostly **boardslides** and a few 360s. But Huston was only 10 years old and skating in front of a large crowd. It was a winning performance.

Huston built on his success. He joined the Dew Tour, an extreme sports competition, in 2006. He landed four top-five finishes in the **park competition**.

Huston talked about his goals during the Dew Tour. "I just want to keep learning new things and keep challenging myself," he said. "I like the challenge."

〉〉〉 Huston, age 11, competes in the Skateboard Street competition during X Games 12 in Los Angeles, California.

〉〉〉 Huston practices at a skate park in Denver, Colorado, in 2005.

Raised Rastafarian

Huston was raised as a Rastafarian. Music plays an important role in this religious group. Many Rastafarians also grow their hair into long braids called dreadlocks. Huston had dreadlocks when he was a young skater. Rastafarians also eat very healthy. Huston was raised as a vegan. He didn't eat any food from animals. He has said his diet has protected him as a skateboarder. He believes it is why he has never broken a bone skating.

CHAPTER TWO

DOMINATING THE X GAMES

In 2006, Huston made history when he competed in his first X Games. The extreme sport competition attracts skaters from around the world. Huston was the youngest person ever to compete. He was only 11 years old!

Huston got a lot of attention because of his age. But he also proved he was a superstar skateboarder. His runs were filled with **kickflips** and **ollies**. He hit backside boardslides, a hard trick to land, throughout his routines.

Competing against the best skaters in the world, Huston wasn't expected to win. In the end, he finished in eighth place. But the experience prepared the young skater for many more trips to the X Games.

FACT

By the time he was 12, Huston was earning $300,000 per year as a professional skateboarder.

>>> Huston skates his way to an eighth-place finish at his first X Games appearance in 2006.

KID WONDER

The small kid with the big dreadlocks quickly became one of the best competitive skaters. In 2007, Huston's main **sponsor**, Element, made a series of skating videos of him doing street tricks.

For skaters like Huston, these street videos are a way to get paid while perfecting their latest tricks. They are also an important way to build up a following.

Huston's early videos included him riding the rails down huge sets of stairs. He performed 360 flips over garbage cans and rode high up on concrete walls.

"I have a little bit of a feeling of something I need to prove just as far as people looking at me," he said about making videos, "not just as a contest skater but as a street skater too."

Huston's videos earned millions of views, despite his young age. Those numbers were unheard of at the time.

FACT

Huston earned his first sponsorship with Element, one of the largest skateboard companies in the world, when he was only seven years old.

>>> Huston competes in the Skateboard Street competition during X Games 12.

CHAPTER THREE
FAMILY STRUGGLES

Huston had been an **elite** skateboarder since he was just seven years old. But his bright future seemed threatened when his father made a sudden decision. The family would be moving to a rural farm in Puerto Rico.

". . . my dad wanted to keep his kids isolated from social influences like going to school and making friends," Huston said, explaining the move.

Huston was now thousands of miles away from his friends. Up until the move, he had been earning hundreds of thousands of dollars. Now he sometimes had no electricity or running water.

The move also made training and competing challenging. Huston's huge skate park was gone. His dad built a few ramps to help him train, but Huston missed California.

"All I wanted to do was skate," he wrote in 2015. "San Lorenzo, Puerto Rico, was a long way from the skateboarding life I'd left in California."

〉〉〉 Huston soars through the air while competing in 2008.

LIFE ON THE FARM

Huston continued to skate competitively while living in Puerto Rico. It wasn't easy, though. His father managed his skateboarding career and served as his coach.

Huston traveled to X Games 15 in Los Angeles to compete in 2009.

A couple years later, Huston's mom moved back to California with his siblings. But Huston stayed behind.

"(My dad) wanted to stay in Puerto Rico," Huston said. "Since he was managing my skateboarding career, I stayed with him."

Huston lived in Puerto Rico with his father for roughly two more years. There, he worked on the farm and trained.

›››
Huston, 14, completes a trick during the finals of a street competition in 2012.

Finally, his mom brought him home to California. By then, Huston had been gone for almost four years. Despite the time away, he quickly returned to the top of competitive skateboarding.

FACT

As a child, Huston also lived in Hawaii and Fiji.

CHAPTER FOUR

A ROCKY RETURN

In 2007, Huston returned to X Games 13 in Los Angeles, California. He was still one of the youngest competitors. He hoped to build on his success from 2006.

Instead, the young skater struggled in his return to the sport's biggest stage. Chris Cole, who'd won the gold medal in 2006, repeated as champion. Huston dropped to 11th place.

But Huston didn't quit. Instead, he went back to work. He trained every day. He never gave up. For him, Huston says, skateboarding is about practicing a trick until it is perfect.

Following the 2007 games, Huston worked to perfect his runs. He hoped all his hard work would pay off. He had nothing to worry about.

>>> Huston continued competing after his disappointing performance at X Games 13.

GRABBING THE GOLD

Huston finished second at both the 2009 and 2010 X Games. Finally, in 2011, Huston struck gold at X Games 17. He was in the finals, challenging defending champion Ryan Sheckler.

Huston would need a monster performance if he was going to capture his first X Games gold medal. He opened his final run with a boardslide. Then he completed what one announcer called "by far the best run . . . of the entire weekend."

⟨⟨⟨ Huston grinds a rail at X Games 16.

On Huston's second rail, the 16-year-old launched a perfect 360 flip into a **tailslide**. He stuck a perfect landing.

Huston finished with an overall score of 91.66 (out of 100). It was enough to earn him the gold. He won by just .66 of a point.

FACT

Huston holds the X Games record for most medals in Skateboard Street competition. He has 16 medals: 10 gold, four silver, and two bronze.

〉〉〉 Huston's performance at X Games 16 earned him a silver medal.

CHAPTER FIVE

WORLD SKATEBOARDING CHAMPION

While the X Games get a lot of attention, the World Skateboarding Championship is also huge. Huston is a four-time champion. He won the title three years in a row from 2017–2019.

In 2017, he also competed in the Street League Skateboarding Super Crown World Championship in Los Angeles, California. But Huston had been hospitalized a week earlier after a serious fall. He was skating on an injured ankle.

At first, Huston's ankle seemed to limit him. He fell on his first two runs. But Huston stormed back. His third trick featured a nollie heelflip. He landed it perfectly and earned a 9.3.

Huston followed that up with a 270 kickflip lipside down the rail. The trick earned him a 9.5, the highest score of the year. Though Huston fell again on his fifth run, he had done enough. He was the 2017 SLS World Champion!

FACT

By the time he turned 19, Huston had won more than $2 million in prize money!

⟨⟨⟨ Huston performs a grind while warming up for the X Games in 2017.

SKATEBOARD SUPERSTAR

Expectations were high for Huston in 2018. In July, he topped a talented field at X Games Minneapolis. Huston was recovering from a knee injury, but it didn't stop him. He delivered a 93.0 on his second run. It was enough to win the gold!

Next up was Australia. The country's first X Games event was held in October 2018. Huston was competing against 11 of the best riders in the world. He hoped to win back-to-back X Games gold.

〉〉〉 Huston soars above a rail during practice in Sydney, Australia.

>>> Huston wows the crowd during a
Street League Skateboarding World
Tour event in London, England.

Huston opened the finals with a solid 94.33, but
he wasn't done. His final run thrilled the crowd. It
featured a kickflip to frontside nosegrind on the
bump to rail 360 kickflip over the long fun box. He
continued with a fakie landing on his nollie backside
heelflip down the big rail. The nearly perfect run
earned him a score of 96.00 and another gold medal!

WHAT'S NEXT?

In 2019, Huston built on his X Games success with first-place finishes in Shanghai, China, and Minneapolis, Minnesota. He also added another silver medal in Minneapolis.

So what's next for skateboarding's biggest superstar? Huston is looking ahead to the Summer Olympics in Tokyo, Japan. For the first time in history, skateboarding has been added as an Olympic sport. Huston will lead Team USA.

Huston vs. Hawk

Huston has won 16 X Game medals and earned more money than any skater in history. But is he the greatest skater of all time? Tony Hawk is a legend of skateboarding. He was the first skateboarder to ever land a **900**. He won more than 70 events over his 17-year career. And his Tony Hawk video game has earned more than $1.4 billion. Huston may have some work to do to catch Hawk as the greatest of all time.

"It's a crazy time for skateboarding," Huston said in 2019. "To think it took this long to get into the Olympics. . . . I'm thankful I'm at a point in my career where I can hopefully get out there and represent my country and nail it."

⟨⟨⟨ Huston will help lead Team USA at the Tokyo Olympics in 2021.

ONE OF THE GREATS

How do you decide who is the greatest? Is it who wins the most medals? Who earns the most money? Who tries the craziest tricks?

Huston shows off his love of skateboarding at an event in Tokyo, Japan.

Deciding who is the best in a sport like skateboarding is hard. The sport is filled with great athletes. You get to decide where Nyjah Huston ranks. Is he the greatest American skater? Is he the greatest skater in the world?

One thing is for sure: Huston's style on the board has fueled a huge growth in popularity of skateboarding. It has also made him a hero to millions of fans worldwide!

TIMELINE

1994   Nyjah Huston is born in Davis, California, on November 30.

2005   Huston wins his first competition, the Tampa Am, in Florida.

2008   Huston launches his nonprofit group, Let It Flow, to help communities around the world have clean drinking water.

2011   Huston wins his first X Games gold medal, competing in the street category.

2013   Huston breaks the record for most money earned by a skateboarder in history.

2013   Huston launches his own skate shoe through DC Shoes.

2014   Huston captures his first gold medal at the World Skateboarding Championship in New Jersey.

2015   Huston signs a multiyear sponsorship deal with Nike SB.

2017   Huston is crowned the Street League Skateboarding World Champion!

2019   Huston wins two medals at X Games Minneapolis, giving him a record 16 medals in street skating.

GLOSSARY

360 (three-SIX-tee)—a 360-degree turn done very rapidly

900 (nine-HUHN-druhd)—a skateboarding trick done in the air; the skateboarder makes two-and-a-half turns, ending facing down on the landing

BOARDSLIDE (bohrd-slahyd)—a trick that involves a skateboarder sliding the middle of his or her board on a rail or ledge

ELITE (i-LEET)—the best in the league

KICKFLIP (KIK-flip)—a trick in which a skateboarder flips the board over during an ollie

OLLIE (AH-lee)—a trick in which a skateboarder steps on the back of the board to make the board rise into the air

PARK COMPETITION (pahrk kom-puh-TISH-uhn)—a style of skateboarding that takes place in purpose-built skate parks; it combines half-pipes and quarter pipes with other "street" obstacles like stairs and rails

SPONSOR (SPON-sur)—a person or company that supports an athlete financially in exchange for advertisements

TAILSLIDE (teyl-slahyd)—a slide where a skateboarder does an ollie with the tail of his or her board and lands with the tail on the edge

READ MORE

Carr, Aaron. *Skateboarding*. New York: AV2 by Weigl, 2020.

Castellano, Peter. *Longboard Skateboarding*. New York: Gareth Stevens Publishing, 2015.

Lyon, Drew. *Downhill Skateboarding and Other Extreme Skateboarding*. North Mankato, MN: Capstone Press, 2020.

INTERNET SITES

X Games Skateboarding
www.xgames.com/video/skateboarding

Street League Skateboarding
streetleague.com

Nyjah Huston's Official Website
nyjah.com

INDEX